Printed
Portraits

Printed Portraits

Clifford S. Ackley

Associate Curator
Department of Prints, Drawings, and Photographs

Museum of Fine Arts

Boston

Copyright © 1979 by the Museum of Fine Arts,
Boston, Massachusetts
Library of Congress Catalog Card no. 79-52929
ISBN 0-87846-139-6
Typeset by Wrightson Typographers, Newton, Massachusetts
Printed by The Meriden Gravure Co., Meriden, Connecticut
Designed by Carl Zahn

Frontispiece:

Antonie van Dyck, Flemish, 1599–1641
Self-Portrait
Etching, first state, about 1640–41
Gift of the Visiting Committee, M26258

Title page:

Rembrandt van Rijn, Dutch, 1606–1669
Self-Portrait
Etching, 1630
Harvey D. Parker Collection. P381

Printed
Portraits

This picture essay on expressive portraiture in
prints and photographs is based on an exhibition
held in the Print and Drawing Galleries of the
Museum of Fine Arts from November 10, 1972,
to January 24, 1973. The exhibition was the first
in a series, which included "Printed Landscapes"
and "The Light in the Interior," that brought
together in new thematic relationships prints and
photographs from all periods in the museum's
permanent collection.

The present essay explores by juxtaposition such
themes as the self-portrait, the symbolic frame,
the ruler portrait, caricature, and the expressive
use of distortion, simplification, and abstraction.
It is published on the occasion of the first exhibition of the Museum of Fine Arts at Faneuil Hall.

In the preparation of this picture book I was
assisted by the staff and volunteers of the Department of Prints, Drawings, and Photographs and
by the staff of the museum's library and office
of publications.

C.S.A.

1   ISRAHEL VAN MECKENEM, German, 1445–1503
The Artist and His Wife, Ida
Engraving, about 1490
Harriet Otis Cruft Fund. M28128

*Israhel van Meckenem's portrait of himself and his wife, Ida, is
the earliest Western printed portrait as well as the earliest printed
self-portrait. The subjects are identified in the Latin inscription
in the lower margin.*

2 ANTONIE VAN DYCK, Flemish, 1599–1641
Self-Portrait
Etching, first state, about 1640–41
Gift of the Visiting Committee, M26258

3 REMBRANDT VAN RIJN, Dutch, 1606–1669
Self-Portrait
Etching, 1630
Harvey D. Parker Collection. P381

Van Dyck's elegant, almost foppish, self-portrait etching contrasts sharply with the young Rembrandt's scowling Bohemian self-image. The Van Dyck is one in a large series of portraits of famous men designed by him to be reproduced by professional engravers. This is one of the few plates in the series etched by Van Dyck himself, and only this stage is entirely his, for the plate was completed by a professional engraver.

4   MARC CHAGALL, born Russia 1889, active France
Self-Portrait with Grimace
Etching and aquatint, 1924–25
George Peabody Gardner Fund. 1960.10

5   JOAN MIRÓ, Spanish, born 1893, and
    LOUIS MARCOUSSIS, born Poland, active France 1883–1941
    Portrait of Miró
    Engraving and drypoint, 1938
    Lee M. Friedman Fund. 1970.51

This surrealist portrait of the Spanish painter Joan Miró was begun by the French painter Louis Marcoussis in engraving and completed by Miró in drypoint. The fragmentary poetic French phrases at the lower left, "pluie de lyres" and "CIRQUES DE MELANCOLIE," may be translated as "rain of lyres" and "circuses of melancholy."

6   PAUL CÉZANNE, French, 1839–1906
    Self-Portrait
    Lithograph, 1896–97
    Bequest of W. G. Russell Allen. 1960.80

7   MAX BECKMANN, German, 1884–1950
    Self-Portrait in Hotel
    Lithograph, 1922, first print in the portfolio *Berliner Reise*
    (*Berlin Journey*)
    Lee M. Friedman Fund. 1965.1323

9/100   Beckmann

8   CAMILLE PISSARRO, French, 1830–1903
    Self-Portrait
    Etching, about 1890
    Lee M. Friedman Fund. 1960.249

9   EDGAR DEGAS, French, 1834–1917
    The Engraver Joseph Tourny (1817–1880)
    Etching, printed in brown on oriental paper, 1856
    Bequest of W. G. Russell Allen. 1960.256

*These two etched portraits by French impressionist painters are
both indebted to the seventeenth-century painter and etcher
Rembrandt, whose influence was so pervasive in nineteenth-
century printmaking.*

Käthe Kollwitz

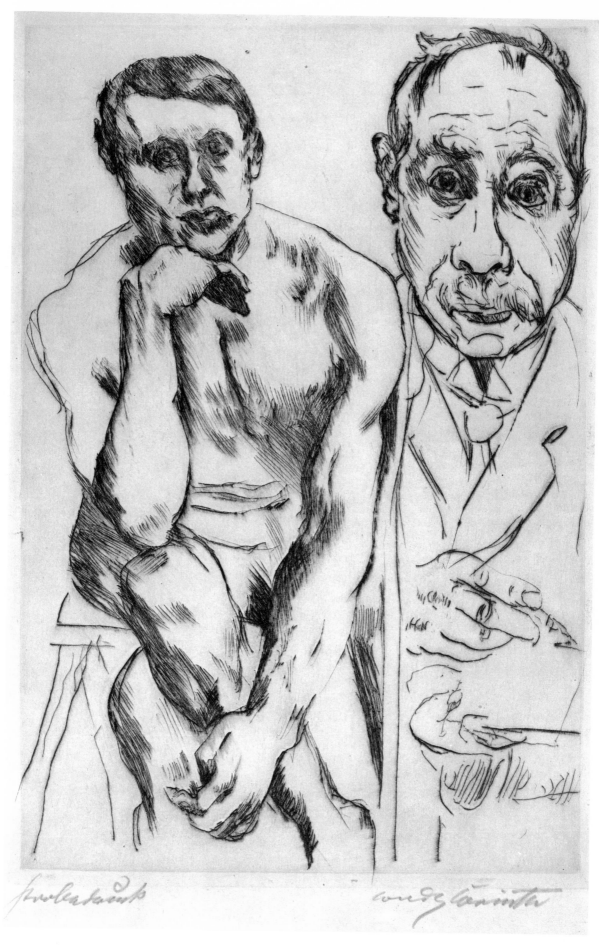

13 LOVIS CORINTH, German, 1858–1925
Self-Portrait with Model
Drypoint, 1917
George Peabody Gardner Fund. 1959.667

10 KÄTHE KOLLWITZ, German, 1867–1945
   Self-Portrait
   Etching and aquatint, about 1893
   Lee M. Friedman Fund. 1966.197

11 KÄTHE KOLLWITZ, German, 1867–1945
   Self-Portrait
   Lithograph on oriental paper, 1904
   Frederick Brown Fund. 1955.227

12 KÄTHE KOLLWITZ, German, 1867–1945
   Self-Portrait
   Woodcut, 1923
   Bequest of W. G. Russell Allen. 1961.27

*Like other Northern European artists such as Rembrandt, van
Gogh, and Beckmann, the German printmaker Käthe Kollwitz
executed numerous self-portraits throughout her career. Her
self-image is seen here in three different print media at three stages
of her life.*

14 MASTER I. B., German, active about 1525–1530
Philipp Melanchthon
Engraving, 1530
Harvey D. Parker Collection. P860

15 ALBRECHT DÜRER, German, 1471–1528
Philipp Melanchthon
Engraving, 1526
Stephen Bullard Memorial Fund. 1968.238

Philipp Melanchthon, a theologian who was a close collabor
of the sixteenth-century religious reformer Martin Luther, is
portrayed here in two prints by Nuremberg artists: Albrecht
Dürer, Nuremberg's greatest artist, and a humbler contempo
the anonymous monogrammist "I.B." Dürer's idealized port
stresses the visionary qualities of Melanchthon while "I.B."
sents the plain facts of the theologian's appearance.

1526
VIVENTIS·POTVIT·DVRERIVS·ORA·PHILIPPI
MENTEM·NON·POTVIT·PINGERE·DOCTA
MANVS

·ER·ROT·

TERMINVS

Corporis effigiem si quis non uidit Erasmi,
Hanc scite aduiuum picta tabella dabit.

HANS HOLBEIN, German, 1497–1554
Desiderius Erasmus
Woodcut, about 1535
Gift of Mr. and Mrs. Edward Wheelright. M21338

e *great sixteenth-century Dutch humanist and scholar (1469–*
6) stands in a kind of triumphal arch, his hand resting on the
d of a figure of Terminus, the ancient Roman god of bounda-
s and endings. For Erasmus, who took the image of the god as
personal emblem, Terminus served as a reminder of the immi-
t end of human existence and an admonition to live a better life.

17 JACQUES CALLOT, French, active Italy, 1592–1635
Giovanni Domenico Peri, poet
Etching and engraving, 1620
Katherine Eliot Bullard Fund. 1963.1266

The portrait of the Italian poet Giovanni Domenico Peri (1564–
1639), who came from peasant stock and who preferred to live
a rural life, has been provided by Callot with an appropriately
symbolic frame composed of cattle and farm implements. The
plate appeared as the author's portrait in a volume of Peri's poetry
in 1620.

18 MICHIEL VAN MUSSCHER, Dutch, 1645–1705
  Self-Portrait with Symbols of Time and Transience
  Mezzotint, proof before the edition, 1685
  Stephen Bullard Memorial Fund. 1969.1237

*In the published version of this rather pompous self-portrait by
a minor Dutch painter, the verses engraved on the tablet indicate
that Time raises the curtain to reveal the greatness of Musscher,
while extending an hourglass to remind him that his time has
almost run out. The child blowing soap bubbles at the left was a
popular seventeenth-century emblem of the fragility of human life.*

19 REMBRANDT VAN RIJN, Dutch, 1606–1669
  Jan Cornelisz. Sylvius, preacher
  Etching and drypoint, 1646
  Gift of William Norton Bullard. 23.1017

*In Rembrandt's posthumous portrait of Jan Cornelisz. Sylvius
(1564–1638) the preacher's eloquence seems to transcend the
grave. Sylvius, vividly gesturing, leans out of an oval opening
cut in a frame that suggests the memorial tablets set into church
walls in Rembrandt's time. Sylvius was the guardian of Rembrandt's wife, Saskia.*

Spes mea Christus. Iohannes Cornelij Sylvius. Amstelodamobat: functus S.S. Minist: ãos 45. et 6. menses. In Frysiã, in Tyenarum et Phrisdum ãos 4. In Balc et Harich unicum. Ia Munsterag. ãos 4...

...Novembr. natus ãos 74.

Hollandiæ Slotis ãos 6. Amstelodami ãos 28. et 6. menses, ibidemq obijt ãõ 1638. 19.

Cuius adorandum docuit Facundia Christum,
   Et populis veram pandit ad astra viam.
Talis erat Sylvî facies. audivimus illum
   Amstelÿs isto civibus ore logui.
Hoc Frisÿs præcepta dedit; pietasq severo
   Relligioq diu vindice tuta stetit.
Praluxit, veneranda suis virtutibus, ætas.
   Erudytq ipsos sessa senecta viros.

Simplicitatis amans sucum contemsit honesti,
   Nec sola voluit fronte placere bonis.
Sic statuit: Iesum vita meliore doceri
   Rectius, et vocum fulmina posse minus.
Amstela, sis memor extincti. qui condidit urbem
   Moribus, hanc ipso fulsÿt illo Deo.
                     C. Barlæus.
Haud amplius deprædico illius dotes,
   Quas æmulor, frustraque perseguor versu.
                       P. S.

20 CORNELIS MASSYS, Flemish, before 1508–after 1560
Henry VIII, King of England (1491–1547)
Engraving, dated in reverse upper right 1544 and at left 1548
Harvey D. Parker Collection. P9227

The portrait by the Flemish engraver conveys Henry's love of good living and a certain slyness of expression.

21 LUCAS VAN LEYDEN, Dutch, 1494–1533
Emperor Maximilian I (1459–1519)
Etching and engraving, 1520
William Francis Warden Fund. 1948.3

The Holy Roman emperor, the Hapsburg Maximilian I (1459–1519), who died the year before this print was executed, was popular with artists because of the many commissions he gave them during his lifetime. Lucas based his portrait on an Albrecht Dürer drawing from life that was available to him in the form of woodcuts after the drawing.

MARIE-ANT.ᵗᵉ D'AUTRICHE, Reine de France et de Navarre.

22 FRANÇOIS JANINET, French, 1752–1814
    Marie Antoinette, Queen of France (1755–1793)
    Color intaglio on two sheets of paper (frame separately
    printed) with additional hand-applied color and gold, 1777
    John B. How Bequest. M36111

*The pleasure-loving and extravagant Marie Antoinette, daughter
of Maria Theresa of Austria and wife of Louis XVI of France, is
seen here at the height of her worldly glory. The effect of this
official portrait is heightened by the subtlety of its blue and gold
coloring. The separately printed frame, resembling the carved
and gilded frame of a painting, epitomizes the style of furniture
known as "Marie Antoinette."*

23 WILLIAM ROGERS, English, active 1589–1604
    Elizabeth I, Queen of England (1533–1603)
    Engraving, about 1595–1600, after a drawing
    by Isaac Oliver, miniaturist
    Horatio Greenough Curtis Fund. 1945.771

*Usually adorned like a holy image to convey the majesty of her
position, Elizabeth, referred to by poets as "Gloriana," possess
an enormous wardrobe of richly embroidered court and state
gowns.*

Th'admired Empresse through the worlde applauded, Unto the eares of every forraigne Nation
For supreme Virtues rares & Imitation: Cannopey'd under powreful Angells winges
Whose Scepters rule fames lowde-voyc'd trumpet lawdeth, To her Immortall praise sweete Science singes

Are to be sould in Popes head Alley by Io Sudbury and Geor Humble.

POT-DE-NAZ

24 HONORÉ DAUMIER, French, 1808–1879
Pot-De-Naz (Joseph, Baron de Podenas)
Lithograph, as published in *Charivari*, 14 June 1833
Bequest of William P. Babcock. B4197

Members of the French parliament were portrayed with savage satire by the painter and caricaturist Daumier. The politician's name has been slightly altered to protect the cartoonist, who had been previously jailed, from prosecution.

25 JOSIAH JOHNSON HAWES, American, 1808–1901
Daniel Webster, statesman, orator
Photograph, albumen print, 1886, enlarged detail from a daguerreotype of 1850
Bequest of W. G. Russell Allen. 1978.154

An enlarged detail from an earlier daguerreotype of 1850 made by Hawes for the Boston firm of Southworth and Hawes preserves for posterity the eagle-like features of Daniel Webster, the controversial statesman and orator. The politician's craggy bone structure contributed enormously to the effect of his public speeches.

26 WALTER SICKERT, English, 1860-1942
   Vision, Volumes and Recession (the art critic
   Roger Fry, lecturing)
   Etching, 1920s
   Stephen Bullard Memorial Fund. 1958.545

The English painter and critic Roger Fry (1866-1934), a vigorous defender of French modernism in art, seen here while lecturing, has been portrayed by the English painter and etcher Sickert as Don Quixote.

27 GIOVANNI BATTISTA PIRANESI, Italian, 1720-1778
   Niccolò Zabaglia, engineer of St. Peter's
   Etching, printed in brown and black, 1764, after a drawing
   by Pier Leone Ghezzi dated 1748
   Gift of Philip Hofer. 1965.1714

An etching by the Italian architect and etcher Piranesi, after a drawing by the Italian caricaturist Ghezzi (1674–1755), suggests that Zabaglia (about 1664–1750), chief of construction at St. Peter's, Rome, had a strong penchant for food and drink.

Cav: Piranesi. Sc:

Sig.re Nicola Zabbaglia Ingegnere della Reverenda
Fabbrica di S. Pietro.

28 JAMES A. MCNEILL WHISTLER, born United States, active
    England and France, 1834–1903
    Charles Drouet, sculptor and collector
    Drypoint, 1859
    Frederick Keppel Memorial Fund. M23406

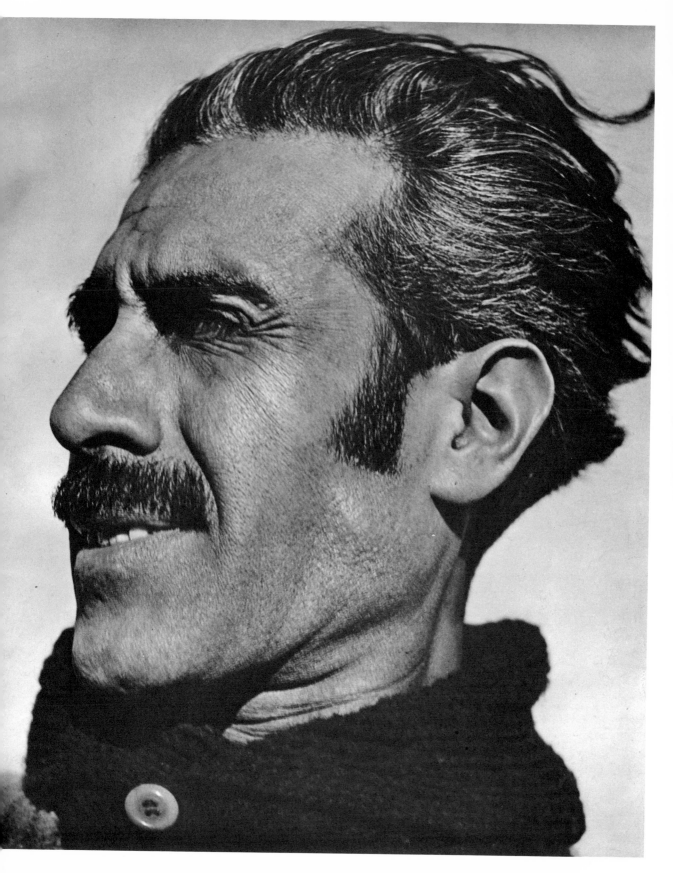

EDWARD WESTON, American, 1886–1958
Galván shooting
Photograph, 1924
Mary L. Smith Fund. 1970.480

of the "heroic heads" made by the American photographer
ard Weston during his Mexican period represents his friend
Mexican senator Manuel Hernandez Galván, a crack shot, in
ct of firing a pistol.

30 EDGAR DEGAS, French, 1834–1917
   Marguerite De Gas
   Etching, about 1865
   Katherine Eliot Bullard Fund. 1973.2

Marguerite De Gas (1842–1895) was the painter's younger sister.

Imp.Lemercier & Cie,Paris

31 EDOUARD MANET, French, 1832–1883
   Berthe Morisot, painter (1841–1895)
   Lithograph, 1872
   Gift of Samuel Putnam Avery. M5849

*The painter Berthe Morisot was the painter Edouard Manet's
sister-in-law.*

32 PAUL GAUGUIN, French, 1848–1903
Stéphane Mallarmé, poet
Etching, 1891
Bequest of W. G. Russell Allen. 1960.317

33 EDVARD MUNCH, Norwegian, active France and Germ
1863–1944
Stéphane Mallarmé, poet
Lithograph, 1896
William Francis Warden Fund. 1957.669

35 ODILON REDON, French, 1840–1916
Edouard Vuillard, painter (1868–1940)
Lithograph, 1900
Bequest of W. G. Russell Allen. 1960.718

34 JAMES A. McNEILL WHISTLER, born United States, active
England and France, 1834–1903
Stéphane Mallarmé, poet
Lithograph, 1892
Gift of Francis Bullard. M21090

The symbolist poet Stéphane Mallarmé (1842–1898) was a cen-
tral figure of artistic and literary life in Paris in the late nineteenth
century. The Whistler lithograph served as a frontispiece for a
collection of the poet's writings published in 1894. In Gauguin's
etching the head of a raven is visible behind the poet, an allusion
to Mallarmé's translation into French of Edgar Allan Poe's poem
The Raven.

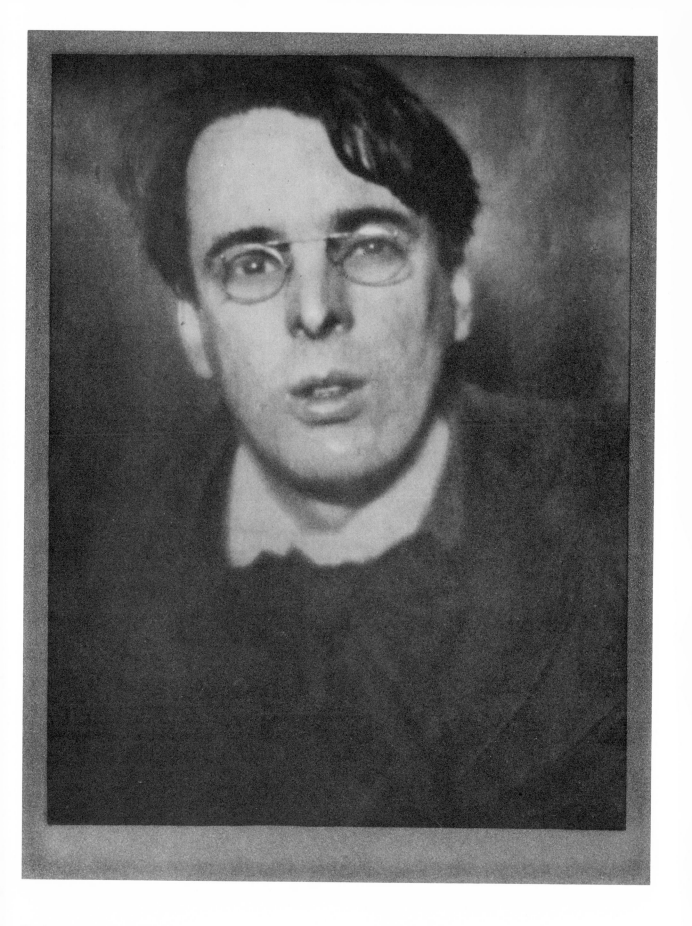

36 EUGÈNE CARRIÈRE, French, 1849–1906
   Paul Verlaine, poet (1844–1896)
   Lithograph, 1896
   Harriet Otis Cruft Fund. 1937.516

37 ALVIN LANGDON COBURN, born United States, active
   England 1882–1966
   William Butler Yeats, poet (1865–1939)
   Photogravure, 1913, from *Men of Mark*
   Benjamin P. Cheney Fund. 1972.219

38 REMBRANDT VAN RIJN, Dutch, 1606–1669
Clement de Jonghe, print publisher
Etching, first state, 1651
Harvey D. Parker Collection. P642

39 REMBRANDT VAN RIJN, Dutch, 1606–1669
Clement de Jonghe, print publisher
Etching and drypoint, third state, 1651
William Francis Warden Fund. 1948.5

*Rembrandt's portrait of Clement de Jonghe, the Amsterdam
print publisher (active from 1640, died 1679), is seen in two stages
of development: the first state, which conveys the feeling of a
straightforward sketch from life, and the third state, which is
more generalized and more introspective, provoking speculation
about the mysteries of human personality.*

40 PABLO PICASSO, born Spain, active France, 1881–1973
   Ambroise Vollard, dealer and publisher
   Etching, 1937
   The Otis Norcross Fund. 1956.29

41 PABLO PICASSO, born Spain, active France, 1881–1973
   Ambroise Vollard, dealer and publisher
   Aquatint, 1931
   The Otis Norcross Fund. 1956.31

42 PIERRE BONNARD, French, 1867–1947
   Ambroise Vollard, dealer and publisher
   Etching, about 1914
   George Peabody Gardner Fund. 1954.666

*Ambroise Vollard, the great French art dealer and a leading pub-
lisher of original prints and of artist-illustrated books, is seen
in two of the three portraits etched by Picasso to accompany
Vollard's edition of ninety-seven other Picasso etchings of the
1930s. Completed shortly before Vollard's death in 1939, this
edition is traditionally known as the "Vollard Suite." A controversial but influential figure, Vollard was a frequent subject for
artists of the School of Paris.*

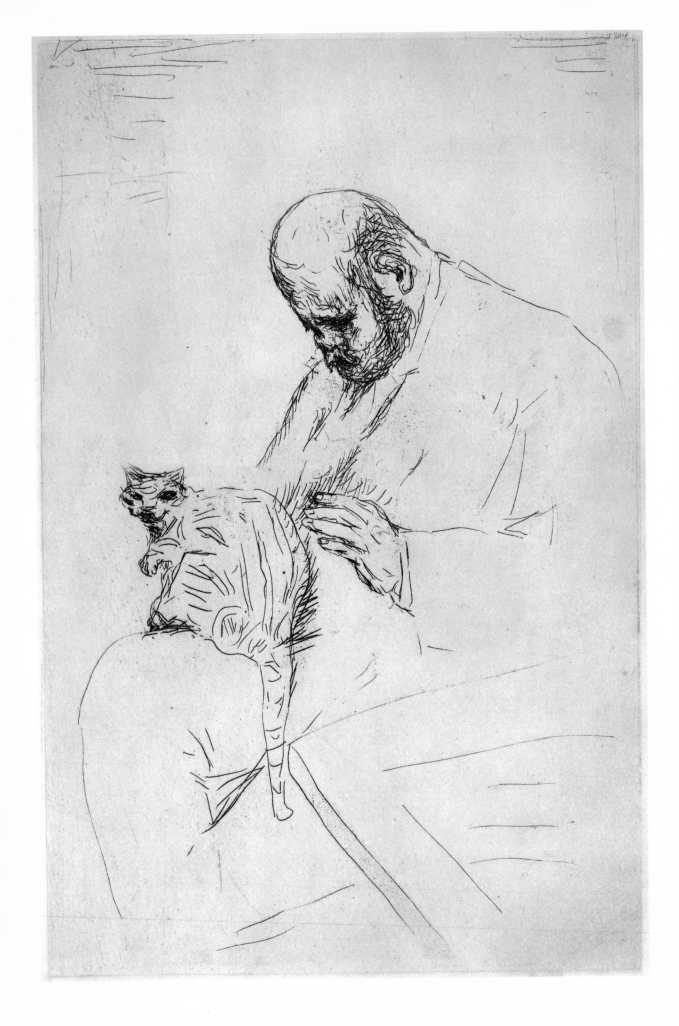

43 HENRI MATISSE, French, 1869-1954
    Charles Bourgeat, engraver (1878-1945)
    Etching, 1914
    Gift of George Peabody Gardner. M28131

44 LOUIS MARCOUSSIS, born Poland, active France, 1883-1941
    Darius Milhaud, composer (1892-1974)
    Engraving, 1936
    The Otis Norcross Fund. 1956.19

Two examples of economy of line in twentieth-century portrai-
ture are illustrated here: the sensitive, quivering etched line of
Matisse and the precise, taut engraved line of Marcoussis.

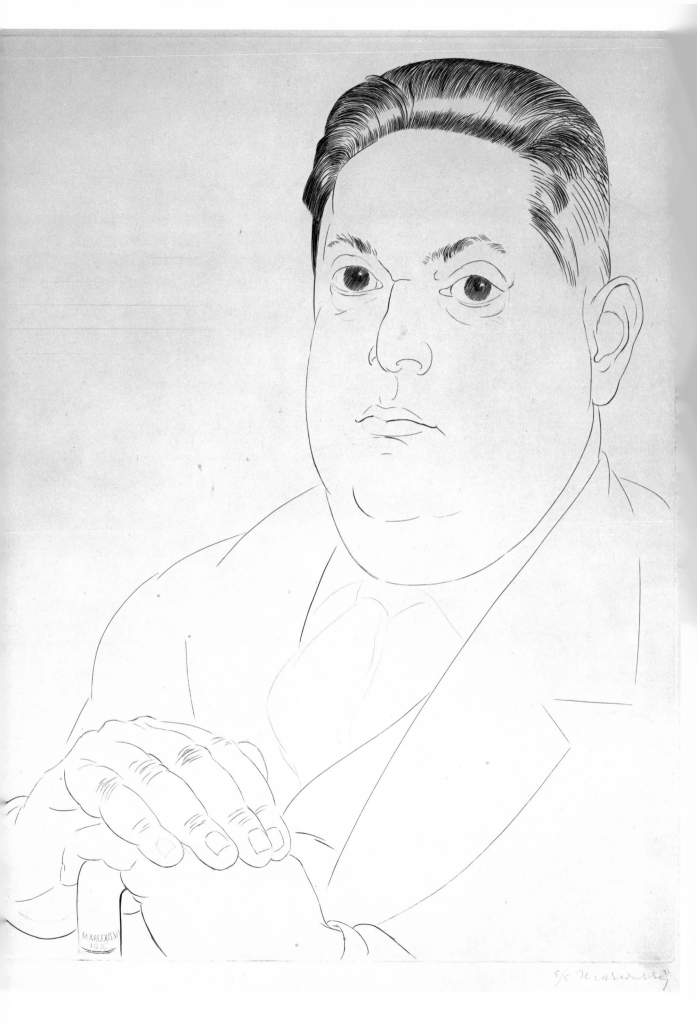

45 Vincent van Gogh, Dutch, active France, 1853–1890
  Dr. Gachet, physician and collector
  Etching, printed in red-brown, May 1890
  Bequest of W. G. Russell Allen. 1960.393

*Dr. Paul Gachet (1828–1909) was a French physician, amateur
artist, collector, and friend of the impressionist painters. The
deeply disturbed Dutch painter van Gogh executed this portrait,
his only etching, in the month that he arrived to stay with Gachet
and to be cared for by him. Two months later, while still Gachet's
guest, he fatally shot himself.*

37/100   Milton Avery 1939

46 MILTON AVERY, American, 1893–1965
Sally with Beret (the artist's wife)
Drypoint, 1939
George P. Nutter Fund. 1970.349

47 JACQUES VILLON (Gaston Duchamp), French, 1875–1963
Yvonne D.
Drypoint, 1913
Bequest of W. G. Russell Allen. 1960.1283

Villon's drypoint is a cubist impression of his sister, Yvonne Duchamp.

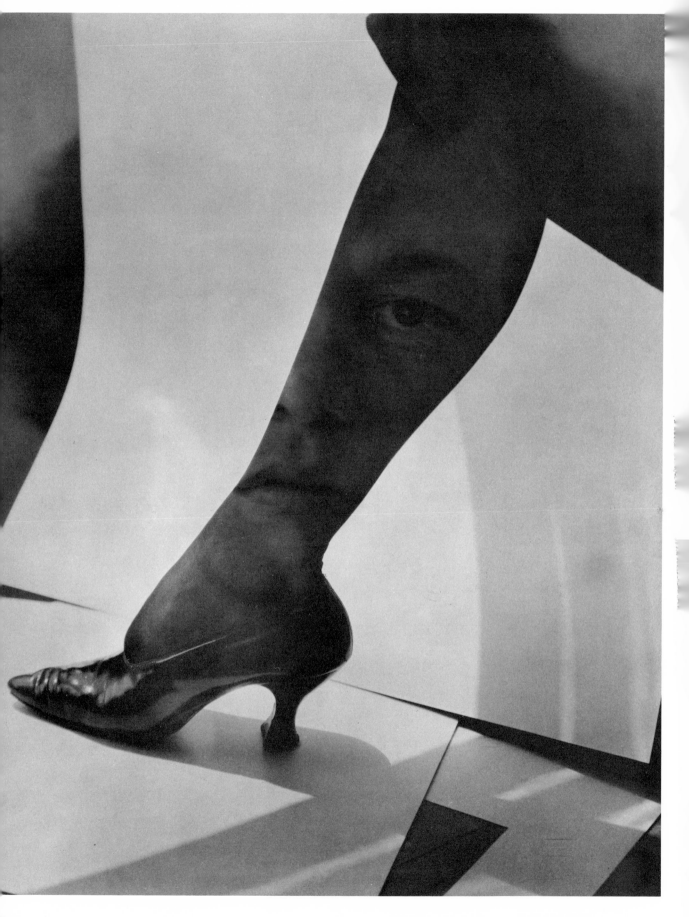

ALFRED STIEGLITZ, American, 1864–1946
Dorothy True
Photograph, 1919
Gift of Alfred Stieglitz, 1924.1720

The great American photographer's "cubist" portrait of a young woman was a happy accident resulting from double exposure while Dorothy True was serving as a model.